SECRET CUTS

SECRET CUTS

A Very Cherry Mystery

by Mardi Link

Cherry orchard in Yuba, Michigan.

This is how you kill a northern Michigan cherry tree: Give it a bacterial canker, which will often kill the blossoms first, then ooze and linger, eventually deforming the rest of the tree.

Infect it with the fungus, Monolinia fructicola, causing brown rot and decaying much of its fruit, sometimes within twenty-four hours.

Send it a bit of Cherry Leaf Spot, which will turn healthy green leaves a sickly yellow, defoliate the entire tree and starve the roots, rendering it helpless over the long winter. Cherry Leaf Spot isn't fazed by snow, ice, or cold. It overwinters easily in its host, enjoying the cold damp, waiting to infect nearby trees come spring.

Unleash a swarm of pests that have a particular craving for its sweet and/or tart leaves, bark, and fruit: for example, the Cherry Lacebug, the Black Cherry Aphid, and myriad varieties of Cherry Fruit Flies – the Europeans, the Easterns, the Blacks, and the Westerns. Follow that with the woodborers, the leaf miners, the leafhoppers, and the chafers.

You could also invite the ravenous Eastern Tent Worm Caterpillar to set up camp in the tree's orchard.

If that doesn't work, then while scientists, horticulturists and politicians debate the specter of global climate change, have the tree endure a couple of freakish winter thaws, a heavy spring blizzard unlike anything recalled in the last half century, a June heat wave and a summer-long drought. And have these weather anomalies all occur within the same growing season.

Or, if the tree has been well cared for by a young cherry farmer, and has managed to grow and thrive for six years despite all of the above biological and meteorological threats, and if the tree was just about to produce its first crop of salable fruit, and if you really did want to kill it dead, why not just have an anonymous coward sneak into the orchard at night and cut it down with a Sawzall.

Cruelly enough, that's exactly what happened to hundreds of young tart cherry trees grown by Traverse City cherry farmers, Mike and Laurie Kroupa.

As best the police can figure, after full dark sometime between Wednesday, October 5, and Tuesday, October 11, 2011, someone drove down M-72 with malice on his or her mind and a sharp saw resting on a backseat, hidden in the trunk of a car, or maybe stashed in the bed of a pickup truck. The driver turned into Legacy Orchards' long grass driveway, followed it to the back of the Kroupas' 110-acre orchard, parked, and shut off the lights.

They grabbed the saw, got out, and began.

Perhaps they were all alone as they worked from tree to tree, carrying out their twisted errand. Perhaps they had help. Either way by daylight 428 cherry trees had been destroyed, each slim healthy trunk cut part way through and then the whole tree pushed over like a broken toothpick.

Courtesy of Grand Traverse County Sheriff's Office.

Courtesy of Grand Traverse County Sheriff's Office.

Nearly a year later, police still have no leads, no motive, no witnesses, very little physical evidence, and no suspect. The cuts didn't even leave wood chips behind, just a little sawdust. The vandal or vandals left no visible footprints in the orchard and by the time police were called to the scene, the vehicle's tire tracks had already been rained on and all but obliterated. Fingerprinting the trees themselves turned out to be impossible.

Mike Kroupa discovered the crime when he was working in his orchard on October 12, 2011, a Wednesday. He immediately called his dad, Gary, and Gary called Grand Traverse County Sheriff's deputy, Justin Revnell. The Kroupas hadn't needed the law much, but Deputy Revnell was their obvious choice when they did; before he became a deputy, Revnell worked full time for the Kroupas in their orchards, doing whatever needed doing. Even after he was hired by the Sheriff's office, he still helped with orchard work when he could, so when Gary described the four to five acre area of the orchard that had been cut down, Revnell knew the exact trees his boss was talking about.

The trio spent hours walking down row after row of dying tart cherry trees, inspecting the damage. Thinking as both an orchard worker and a cop, Revnell's first question, was, "Who?" Later he would spend endless months wondering, "Why?"

"At first you run through the list of possibilities and think, 'It has got to be stupid kids.' Then you do the math. At a minute a tree, there's over seven hours of work there. Kids just don't have that kind of attention span."

Looking down destroyed rows of once neatly planted trees, Revnell couldn't help but think of the economic damage – the trees hadn't even produced a crop yet, they were only six years old and too young to set much fruit, but they still required the same costly and labor-intensive pruning, mowing, spraying, and fertilizing as mature trees would. Revnell asked Mike if Legacy Orchards had any disgruntled employees, but the farmer just shook his head no. His workers weren't just his employees, he said, they were his friends. They would be the last people to do something like this. They loved the land, loved working outside, were nothing but loyal to the Kroupa family.

"He reiterated he had no idea who may have done something like this," Revnell would later write in his police report. "All of his current and past employees are either family or friends and (he) does not believe that any of them would be upset with him or would have done anything like this to him."

Plus, assaulting the trees would be tantamount to financial suicide; this part of the orchard was young, with many good years ahead, and would need workers to help care for it. Employees wouldn't want to end their own jobs, would they? Especially when Michigan's economy was so bad and jobs were few.

Revnell took a walk and knocked on some doors, hoping for a lead. But the orchard's few neighbors were just as shocked by the crime as the Kroupas; to a one they hadn't seen anything, hadn't heard anything. Fellow Cherry farmer Roger Noonan, one of the Kroupas' neighbors to the west, remembers feeling almost sick when he first heard.

"Whoever it was, they knew what they were doing," he said, "And they knew what time to do it."

Tire tracks leading from area of destruction.
Courtesy of Grand Traverse County Sheriff's Office.

Back in his cruiser, Revnell recalled a few hazy details about other recent incidents of farm vandalism in Leelanau, a neighboring county. When he checked with the Leelanau County Sheriff's Office, those details became disturbingly clear: Fifteen cherry trees were cut and pushed over at one orchard and twenty-two at another. And at a nearby vineyard, 161 grapevines were destroyed. Leelanau County Sheriff Mike Oltersdorf confirmed that those cases were also unsolved, with no good leads.

"Somebody had it out for somebody, that's for sure," he said.

The cuts at all three places were eerily similar to those discovered at Kroupas' Legacy Orchards. Did northern Michigan have a serial fruit tree vandal, roaming through orchards in the night, saw in hand? Revnell feared the worst.

In order to fully understand Deputy Justin Revnell's dread, you have to understand the relationship between cherries and northern Michigan. Because, as bad as these crimes were, this wasn't just an attack on a few orchards; this was an attack on a way of life. Cherry farming is essential to the history of Old Mission and Leelanau Peninsulas, and its practice is engaged with so much fervor, the avocation just about approaches a religion.

Adding to this similarity? The domestic cherry arrived in the region at pretty much the same time as the Holy Bible did.

Orchard on Old Mission, overlooking Power Island.
Courtesty History Center of Traverse City.

Vineyard on Old Mission, overlooking Power Island.

The region's agricultural history unfolds like this: Against all advice, in the spring of 1852 it was a missionary, the Rev. Peter Dougherty, who planted the first cherry trees on Old Mission Peninsula. Until the good Reverend arrived on the shore of this 18-mile twig of land jutting into Grand Traverse Bay, Indian farmers relied on hardy and native apple trees to augment their diet, and were skeptical of the thin-limbed cherry. How could something so delicate withstand northern Michigan's harsh winters? Whether because of faith, luck, solid rootstock, or some combination of the three, Rev. Dougherty's trees survived that winter and many that followed it. They grew, and eventually bore fruit.

ev. Peter Dougherty was a 33- year old East Coast educated Presbyterian, sent by his church fathers to Michigan's then exotic-seeming pine plains, cedar swamps, and timber forests. His assignment: Bestow upon local Indians, "a knowledge of the Savior," whether, it's clear in hindsight, the tribes wanted that knowledge or not.

But after a decade at his task the settlement Rev. Dougherty founded on Old Mission Peninsula included a mission church offering regular Sunday services, a mission house which had the distinction of being the first wood framed building in Grand Traverse County, and a school where some forty-eight Indian and white children learned to read, write, farm and to properly care for their tools.

There were also several stores, a post office, and dozens of hewn log houses, whitewashed in an effort to make them distinct from traditional wigwams. Nearby, individual gardens of several acres flourished with potatoes, corn, and squash.

THE FIRST MISSION HOUSE AT OLD MISSION

Rev. Peter Dougherty and his mission. Photos courtesy History Center of Traverse City.

Later, the Reverend would encounter magnificent Indian-grown apple trees with trunks, "as wide as a man's body," and dirt of an extraordinary richness.

"The soil of the table land and its declivities is boulder drift of great thickness, in some places being fifty feet in depth," he wrote in a letter to the Presbyterian Church's mission council. It wasn't the quality of the soil, however, that concerned the Indians who warned the Reverend not to plant his cherry trees; it was the unpredictability of the weather. Particularly the winter weather, the freezes and the thaws.

Which does make one wonder. Even though it's taken 150 years for farmers to acknowledge it, maybe those Indians knew what they were talking about after all.

O ver the next 150 years cherry farmers have thrived in northern Michigan, albeit many like Rev. Dougherty before them, by praying for warm and sunny springs, temperate summers, soaking rains that quit before they crack the fruit, breezes that drive pests and diseases away but don't snap off limbs, and rich soil that drains without drying out.

Taken as a whole, those prayers have mostly been answered, if not by a Supreme Being, then by regular and liberal application of chemical fertilizers and pesticides. Though the practice has its detractors, with the help of big agro-science, cherry farming has expanded on Old Mission and Leelanau Peninsulas far beyond Rev. Dougherty's wildest expectations. In 1893, the first commercial cherry orchard was planted near the site of the Reverend's original trees, and by the early 1900's cherries had become the area's number one local crop.

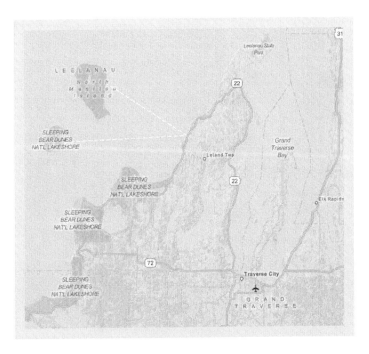

Courtesy MapQuest.

In 1925, an annual sedate and religious "blessing of the blossoms" ceremony morphed into the National Cherry Festival, a spectacle which has attracted U.S. Presidents, Army Generals, a string of state Governors, the U.S. Navy's Blue Angels, Miss America, NASA, the Budweiser Clydesdales, and even the Guinness Book of World Records. (In 1987, a Traverse City bakery made a 28,350-pound cherry pie, the largest ever.)

Hold out your left hand and look at your pinkie fingernail; today that tiny spot of land produces seventy to seventy-five percent of the country's tart cherries – the variety preferred for pies, juice, preserves, garnishes, and cooking – and a whole lot of the country's sweet cherries, too – the variety preferred for fresh eating – earning the Traverse City region the designation of "The Cherry Capital of the World."

The honor has been a long time coming. Since Rev. Dougherty's time, parents have passed their cherry orchards on down to their children, who farm them and then pass them down again. For example, Joseph and Minnie Send started farming eighty acres on Lee Point peninsula just after the turn of the century. When they were ready to retire, the couple sold the farm to their son and daughter-in-law, Joseph Jr. and Rose Send. Over subsequent generations, the farm grew into double its original eighty acres and is now owned by Joseph Jr.'s and Rose's son and daughter-in-law.

A few farmers in the region have sold out to developers, but fervent preservation work by township governments, wealthy area benefactors, and non-profit land conservancies have helped buy up development rights and preserve thousands of acres of family orchards. And with it, regional cherry farming traditions.

So at the dawn of the millennium, despite the pressures of modern life, and despite criticism by those opposed to chemically-supported agriculture, most growers in the know here still believed that cherry farming in northern Michigan had a pretty decent future. Until, that is, the 2012 growing season.

Courtesy History Center of Traverse City.

Courtesy History Center of Traverse City.

By late winter of 2012, the vandalism of 2011 was still an open case for police and a bad memory for farmers. Particularly bad, of course, for the Kroupas, the two orchards vandalized in Leelanau County, and for Crain Hill Vineyards. But then extreme weather in the spring and summer of 2012 devastated not just a few individual farmers, but rather every single cherry farmer in the entire northwestern Michigan region. With the freakish weather on trial and no leads, the vandalism case soon receded into the background. It was officially closed in February 2012.

An early March 2012 snowstorm dropped cement-like drifts that leveled entire trees; that was followed just two weeks later by a freakishly hot and early thaw. The seventy- and even eighty-degree temperatures were far above normal and tricked the remaining healthy trees into blooming more than a month early. Then the region's typical late freezes killed the flowers before they could produce any fruit.

Now it's in the record books: 2012 will go down as the worst year in recorded history for Michigan fruit.

More than ninety percent of the tart cherry crop was killed; estimates released by the Michigan Farm Bureau put dollar amounts at $38.5 million lost for tart cherries and $11.6 million lost for sweets.

"I call it 'Death Valley' now," said Jeff Send, who with his wife, Nita, farms the Send's family's 160 acres plus leases hundreds more with their partners Penny and Scott Emeott.

Many of the Send/Emeott partnership's trees were weakened by the snow, ice, and spring damp and are now succumbing to bacterial canker. Some trees in one low-lying orchard were so far gone they had to be pulled up and destroyed. Across the Grand Traverse Bay to the east, the story is pretty much the same.

Cherry stand on Old Mission, 2012.

"We have no crop," cherry farmer Pat McGuire told a television news reporter for PBS' Newsh Hour broadcast on August 16, 2012. McGuire, along with his wife, Sara, own Royal Farms, an orchard and farm market in Ellsworth that sells dried fruit, cherry concentrate, baked goods, and gift boxes. "We did everything we could to minimize the effects of the weather and still feel like we lost the fight."

And if the weather doesn't get you, there's always the chance that an anonymous coward will sneak into your orchard at night and cut down your trees with a Sawzall.

Uncooperative and even disastrous weather is to be expected in this business. Fruit farmers know that and prepare for it as best they can. Strategies include researching plant varieties, timing the weather, and making the most of region-specific agricultural research. When that fails, there's always crop insurance.

In truly lousy years, many farmers rely on crop insurance pay-outs, which can cover up to eighty-five percent of a farmer's losses, to keep them afloat until the next growing season. That might have helped northern Michigan orchard owners, except that government backed crop insurance isn't available for tart cherry farmers.

No one seems to know why beyond a "we've always done it that way," attitude. That may change, however, if Michigan's U.S. Senator, Debbie Stabenow, gets her way. Stabenow, Chair of the Agriculture, Nutrition and Forestry Committee, worked with the U.S. Department of Agriculture to secure low-interest loans for hard hit Michigan fruit farmers. Her "Agriculture Reform, Food and Jobs Act," also known as the Farm Bill, includes a provision to make crop insurance available to tart cherry farmers for the first time. The Farm Bill passed the Senate 64-35 in June 2012, but as of early September the House had yet to bring it to the floor for a vote.

Michigan tart cherry farmers are hopeful, but political uncertainty still pales in comparison to climate uncertainty.

On July 25, 2012 the *Glen Arbor Sun*, a Leelanau County newspaper, ran this disturbing headline: "Will Climate Change Kill the Michigan Cherry?" In the corresponding article, Sun editor Jacob Wheeler asked the questions increasingly on his readers' minds: "Once cherry farmers stomach their losses and prepare their trees for winter, the elephant in the orchard they'll face is the vexing question of whether this spring's destruction was caused merely by aberrant extreme weather — a 'once-in-a-lifetime freeze-out' — or by global climate change, which could mean warmer winters, more extreme weather events and greater unpredictability."

Like most other places in the country, climate change is a controversial topic here. Some farmers believe it's a reality, while others say its bunk. But if the cherry can't grow here, or grow as abundantly and economically as it has for the past century, farmers won't be the only ones whose livelihood will be put in jeopardy.

A complete supply line of processors, marketers, truckers, wholesale and retail operations have grown up around the prodigious output of northern Michigan cherry orchards and their livelihoods would be threatened as well. Cherry Republic, Benjamin Twiggs, and the Cherry Stop, retailers of cherry-themed food and gifts; Cherry Central, a supplier to food manufacturers:; Cherry Growers, Inc., a grower-owned cooperative fruit processor; and Great Lakes Packing, a family-owned cherry processor, to name a few. Taken together, they represent tens of thousands of northern Michigan jobs.

And it won't take years for these businesses to feel the impact. A few disastrous seasons in a row, like the one just experienced this summer, would do it. For example, Bob Sutherland, owner of Cherry Republic, was forced to import 150,000 pounds of Lutowka cherries from Poland this year just to make the company's pies and other products. He'd much rather buy local, but local farmers had little to sell him.

If another season like this one comes sooner rather than later, more farmers may accept climate change as a reality. But accepting it is just the beginning; figuring out what to do about it is the real challenge. Scientists, bureaucrats, and politicians are working on the "do" part, but no easy answers are forthcoming. No cheap ones, either.

Climatologist, Jeff Andresen, and Michigan State University geography professor, Julie Winkler, co-direct the Pileus Project, which is developing a set of online tools focusing on the influence of weather on tart cherry production.

Amy Iezzoni — the only tart cherry breeder in the country — has been sponsored by MSU to research cold resistance genes in other fruits to see if they can be bred into the tart cherry.

MSU's Leelanau County Research Center Coordinator, Nikki Rothwell, is hoping good old-fashioned debate and discussion will at least spark some ideas. She recently launched a program bringing scientists and researchers together with area growers to discuss immediate, practical solutions to extreme weather. Some of these include frost fans, to circulate cold air in an orchard so it doesn't stagnate on crops, irrigation timed to wet trees so the water freezes and not the fruit, and installing heaters like they do in California orchards. Some of these strategies might work some of the time, but they're expensive. Maybe too expensive to install and still turn a profit on a cherry crop. And if the weather, climate change, damp and drought don't get you, there's always the chance that an anonymous coward will sneak into your orchard at night and cut down your trees with a Sawzall.

he morning after Mike Kroupa discovered so many of his trees were dead or dying, his wife Laura tried to express the couple's feelings about the crime on a regional culinary blog, *Up North Foodies*. It wasn't easy.

"It is impossible to put into words what we are feeling as a result of this devastational [sic] act. These particular trees were only a few years away from being mature enough to harvest. We have lost thousands of dollars in the costs of the trees, as well as in the time and money spent pruning, fertilizing, spraying, and caring for these trees over the last 5 plus years."

Initially, there was a bit of knee-jerk grumbling online and out and about that the crime might be an insurance scam, but the facts soon proved that to be ridiculous. Crop insurance was unavailable for tart cherry farmers like the Kroupas and liability insurance wouldn't cover damage to the trees, only damage to workers. Laura said as much in her blog post.

"Insurance does not believe they will be able to help recover the damage or future loss of income. We will be looking at minimum of an 8 to 9 year setback by the time we are able to plant new trees and get them ready for harvesting. The loss is substantial, not to mention incredibly disheartening, that something like this would happen in our area."

Mike and Laura, along with their neighbor, Roger Noonan, and a few other farmers pooled their resources and offered a $10,000 reward to anyone able to identify the vandal. Days passed with no leads, but plenty of opinion.

Depending upon who you asked, it was a tree-hugger, it was a psycho, it was a migrant worker. It was a competitor, it was drunken teenagers on a dare, it was a ticked off employee. It was corporate real estate developers, it was politics, it was even the Dogman, northern Michigan's answer to Bigfoot.

Local media websites, Facebook, and farming blogs snarled for justice:

"We need the vandals, a bigger tree and a length of rope," someone signed in as "Ed" posted on Facebook.

"When you find them, send them to Afghanistan, not armed!" agreed "Nancy."

On UpNorthLive.com, NBC affiliate 7 & 4's website, someone signed in as "DagnyT" commented, "This was a deliberate malicious act, not just a spur of the moment prank. Angry employee or ex-employee? Can't believe a competitor would do this. Scum of the planet, for certain and I hope he/she/they are caught and prosecuted fully."

Someone calling themselves "AcmePete" predicted, "Gotta believe someone saw something. The perps will eventually open their pie-holes to the wrong person and will be outed . . ."

A full month passed, and still nothing. Then on October 30, 2011, the crime was covered by the state's farming newspaper, *Michigan Farm News*, the first publication to label the crimes "terrorism."

"We had a chat with the sheriff," vineyard owner Robert Brengman told the *News* reporter, "and tried to brainstorm why anyone would want to do this. Maybe they saw a movie about the food industry and how crooked the big players are, and maybe they thought we were part of that and they wanted to get back at a big corporation."

Finally, a lead.

Alittle digging by this author uncovered that six weeks prior to the assault on Crain Vineyards and Legacy Orchards, a compelling documentary film, *If A Tree Falls: A Story of the Earth Liberation Front,* was shown at the Traverse City Film Festival (TCFF). The Film Festival is a popular annual event featuring hundreds of movies and drawing tens of thousands of visitors from around the state, the country, and even the world.

The documentary, *If A Tree Falls,* details the months leading up to the arrest of an accused "eco-terrorist" from the radical environmental group, Earth Liberation Front. It is a gripping and absorbing piece of filmmaking that leaves the viewer feeling conflicted about a system that often sacrifices the health of our natural environment for financial gain. Key to the film's narrative is how an average and seemingly mild-mannered man could turn into a violent environmental crusader.

"Eco-terrorism" is defined by the Federal Bureau of Investigation (FBI) as the "use or threatened use of violence of a criminal nature against people or property by an environmentally oriented, subnational group for environmental-political reasons." It is a controversial term, and some critics have argued that it more accurately describes the actions of polluting and habitat-destroying corporations than of environmental activists. There are several "eco-terrorist"-labeled organizations on the FBI's radar, including the Earth Liberation Front.

More than 150 films were shown at the TCFF in 2011; of those only *If A Tree Falls* won the Festival's coveted Founder's Award. Two weeks after showing at the TCFF, the documentary had its television premiere on the PBS series, "POV." The northern Michigan PBS station, WCMU, subscribes to POV and broadcast

If A Tree Falls on Sept. 13, 2011 at 9 p.m. It was later nominated for an Academy Award for Best Documentary Feature.

Could someone have seen the film locally, once and maybe even twice, then used its emotional story as a catalyst to carry out his or her own twisted version of eco-terrorism? Against northern Michigan cherry farmers?

Initially, that seems implausible. As a writer, a "Friend" of the TCFF, and a regular movie-goer, I don't believe that movies can compel emotionally healthy people to commit crimes. Psychologists generally agree that entertainment such as movies and television shows don't cause crime, though they may appeal to those who already lean in that direction; thinking they are a direct cause is akin to the argument that playing violent video games will turn kids into murderers and listening to rock music leads to drug abuse.

"Movies and games don't put things in people's minds," said one Traverse City area forensic psychologist. "They've got those tendencies in their minds already. They just don't know what to do to act them out." (Concerned about potential retaliation from the vandal, the psychologist, who has consulted with area police departments, declined to have his name in print.)

But then again, hacking down five acres of cherry trees and more than a hundred grapevines in the dead of night would have seemed implausible once, too. Then it really happened.

And, there's something else about that documentary film not so easily dismissed. As the credits roll in *If A Tree Falls*, a haunting and driving song by the indie rock group "The National," plays.

The song is titled "Cherry Tree," and includes these almost prophetic lyrics:

> *Take us down and all apart*
> *Cherry Tree*
> *Lay us out on the table*
>
> *You're sharp all right*
>
> *But no one is asking so leave it alone*
> *Leave it alone*
>
> *Can we show*
> *A little discipline*
> *Can we?*
>
> *Loose lips sink ships*

Courtesy of Grand Traverse County Sheriff's Office.

Ripe and unripe cherries.

A year has passed and there are still no conclusive answers.

"Since the date of this incident, I have received no additional leads and/or information that could lead me to a suspect in this incident," Deputy Revnell wrote in an update to his original police report. "Due to this fact, this incident will be closed. If any additional information comes forward that might help develop a suspect, this incident will be reopened and continue to be investigated."

In a perfect world, this is the point in this journalistic piece where it would be emotionally satisfying for the reader, not to mention this author, to learn the name or names of the guilty. The local forensic psychologist suggested it was a shallow-minded person; someone with an immature personality that went beyond a simple childishness. A person craving recognition because their life felt meaningless.

"He or she is trying to get their life to amount to something and I think they probably had an accomplice with them. Someone to relive the event with. It would take a lot of perseverance to do something like that alone. And while they're acting out they're probably thinking, 'Everyone is going to wonder who did this.' If nobody is going to know who did it, than you wouldn't have anyone to talk to about it with later. To fantasize with. An accomplice would provide that."

That may well be the personality, but it is not the name or names of an actual person. That all-important fact remains elusive. Like the weather, like farming, like history, there is no perfect world and things don't always turn out according to plan. To that end, the $10,000 reward remains unclaimed and this story's investigative reward remains unknown.

"We don't know the 'Who,' and we don't know the 'Why,' either," Deputy Revnell said.

If the case is reopened, it will be Revnell who is again assigned to it. He is still working, off and on when they need him, for the Kroupas.

As for the cherry farmers, they say they know nothing more, that there aren't even any rumors circulating. Which means the vandal either acted alone and told no one, left the area, or did have an accomplice but is holding fast to the song lyric, "Loose lips sink ships."

One man who serves the cherry growing community, spending hours in the orchards talking to farmers, remains stymied, too.

"It's just pretty strange," said chemical rep, Matt Lyons. "The farmers still talk about it, but there's not a single theory that sounds any truer than any other. There's no connection between the growers and the Kroupas are pretty well liked so the idea someone targeted them specifically is weak. I do know one thing. The growers would feel a lot better if we had information that led to the arrest of those people."

The Grand Traverse County Sheriff's Office says tips can be phoned in to the main switchboard, (231) 995-5000, or anonymously to the Silent Observer line, (231) 947-8477.

Cherry orchard, Williamsburg, Michigan.

Maybe this story will spur a memory and a phone call and an arrest. Until then, it will come to an end the very same the way it began. With a list.

This is who might have killed all those northern Michigan cherry trees:

Cherry farmer, Roger Noonan: "I believe it was just one person who did it. Nothing's come out after, and if it was more than one person, someone would have talked. And nobody's talked."

Crain Hill Vineyard owner, Roger Brengman: "An eco-terrorist wannabe."

Leelanau County Sheriff, Mike Oltersdorf: "Personal vendetta. That's the only thing that explains the extent and methodical nature of the damage."

Coordinator of the MSU's Horticultural Research Center, Nikki Rothwell: "I've heard people say it's eco-terrorists, but if that's the case why haven't they claimed responsibility? Those types usually like to make an announcement. But whoever is responsible, it's hard to imagine anyone getting that mad at the very people working to grow the food to feed you."

Cherry farmer Jim Empson: "Snowmobilers who want to ride through the orchards?"

Glen Arbor Sun editor, Jacob Wheeler: "I think it's a fringe person. This was someone who had a bone to pick with a farmer or farmers generally. It's someone who thinks they have a cause."

Anonymous forensic psychologist: "A shallow-minded immature person. Someone who has been made to work in the orchards and never wanted to."

Deputy Justin Revnell: "A nut job."

It is indeed a crazy way to make a living, farming. It has been and probably always will be a profession of hope, hard work and faith.

Still, the resilience of farmers is, out of necessity, boundless. And while there may be any number of ways to kill a cherry tree, or even 428 cherry trees for that matter, those crimes alone won't end cherry farming.

Climate change won't either, if locals and pro-farm politicians have anything to say about it. While Sen. Stabenow's Farm Bill hasn't passed yet, Agriculture Secretary Tom Vilsack did declare all of Michigan's 83 counties a disaster area, making farmers, including tart cherry farmers, eligible for low interest (2.25 percent) loans. Kroupa isn't sure if he'll take out a loan or not, but he is sure Legacy Orchards will continue, despite the vandalism and the climate.

"We've moved on," he said. "Because no matter what, there's always next season."

Shaking cherries at the Ridgewood Farm, Old Mission.

Mardi Link is a writer living in northern Michigan. She is the author of, *When Evil Came to Good Hart*, and *Isadore's Secret*, both published by the University of Michigan Press. I*sadore's Secret* won a Michigan Notable Book Award and was named a, "Great Lakes' Great Read," by the Great Lakes Independent Booksellers Association. Her memoir, *Bootstrapper*, about surviving a year of hardship with her sons on their small hobby farm, will be published by Alfred A. Knopf in 2013.

This investigative piece was funded by Kickstarter.

Thank-you to Daria Alexander, Susan Betts-Barbus, Dorothy Beemsterboer, Sally Bjork, Steven Bollinger, Tobin Buhk, Mary Burton, Brilliant Books, Julie Christensen Spahn, Jerry Dennis, Deborah Diesen, James Filkins, Greifwin, Doug Hansen, Tom Hoffman, Trina Hayes, Kathy Hughes, Mike Hughes, Lynne Hugo, Barbara J., Jerrold Jenkins, Johnny5000, Ron Jolly, Jonny, Linda Joyner, Sylvia Kallemeyn, Richard & Jean Keffer, Larry Kortokrax, Tina Lane, Jim Linderman, Eunice Link, Wayne Lobdell, Donald Lystra, Molly Mahony, John Marsh, Susan & Tim McQuaid, Susan Muldowney, James Muratzki, Gayle Neu, Cari Noga, Agnes K. Ochs, Susan O'Connor, Anne-Marie Oomen, Aaron Peterson, Amos Pollister, Ron, Nancy Ross-Flanigan, Jon Roth, Jack Seaman, Heather Shumaker, Peter Starkel, Ron J. Stefanski, Victoria Sutherland, Sandra Wardwell, Gloria Whelan, Shari & David Wilson, Daniel Winterhalter, Mark Wolfgang, and Deborah Johnson Wood.

Ridgewood Farm, Old Mission, Michigan.

Made in the USA
Charleston, SC
23 September 2012